D1593568

nsure

AHSAHTA PRESS

THE NEW SERIES #37

Pleasure

BRIAN TEARE

AHSAHTA PRESS

BOISE, IDAHO / 2010

Ahsahta Press, Boise State University
Boise, Idaho 83725-1525
http://ahsahtapress.boisestate.edu
http://ahsahtapress.boisestate.edu/books/teare/teare.htm

Copyright © 2010 by Brian Teare
Printed in the United States of America
Cover design by Quemadura
Cover art: undated tintype by unknown photographer from the collection of Robert Flynt
Book design by Janet Holmes
First printing September 2010
ISBN-13: 978-1-934103-16-6

Library of Congress Cataloging-in-Publication Data

Teare, Brian.
Pleasure / Brian Teare.
    p. cm. -- (The new series ; 37)
ISBN-13: 978-1-934103-16-6 (pbk. : alk. paper)
ISBN-10: 1-934103-16-0 (pbk. : alk. paper)
I. Title.
PS3620.E427P54 2010
811'.6--DC22

                    2010020822

ACKNOWLEDGMENTS

Many thanks to the editors and readers of the following journals for their support: The Academy of American Poets online: "Eden Incunabulum"; *Barrow Street*: "Californian (You want to go back)"; *Beloit Poetry Journal*: "To Other Light"; *Boston Review*: "Burnt Text" and "Torn Text" (under the title "from '[Adam] in fragments/with a poem engraved/down the thighs'"); *Legitimate Dangers: American Poets of the New Century*: "Dead House Sonnet"; *New American Writing*: "Of Paradise and the Structure of Gardens"; *NO: A Journal of the Arts*: "Two Elegies Containing Fear"; *Ploughshares*: "The Eden of the Author of Sleep" and "Eden Tiresias"; *Provincetown Arts*: "Dreamt Dead Eden"; *The Seattle Review*: "Californian (It began like this)" and "Californian (The sea begins in regards)"; *Verse*: "Dead House Sonnet"; *VOLT*: "Eden—*pleasure*" (under the title "from '[Adam] in fragments/with a poem engraved/down the thighs'").

For time, money, shelter and community that aided in the completion of this work, my thanks to these institutions: Stanford University, Bucknell University and the Stadler Center for Poetry, the MacDowell Colony, and the National Endowment for the Arts. For help in innumerable ways literary and personal, and in particular support of this work, blessings heaped upon the heads of: Rick Barot, Gaby Calvocoressi, Julie Carr, Joshua Corey, Brenda Hillman, Cynthia Hogue, Jane Mead, Susan Mitchell, D. A. Powell, Margaret Ronda, Reginald Shepherd, Jean Valentine, Kerri Webster, C. D. Wright.

CONTENTS

For J.

In Memoriam

His embrace
was the Law,   *was Syntax.*

—Robert Duncan

DEAD HOUSE SONNET

house of each sentence endlessly hinged, house of each phrase opened elegy
entirely latches, exactly latches, hasps, proliferant, endlessly opened, of doors,
termini effigies, each noun in a house a nova of votives, wicks ashen, burnt
them, syntax like bark that smoldered the garden in winter, nasturtiums
come summer undone verbs, burnt them, burnt tense, the present's past, burnt
that, house of ash, house a tinge, a reek of eucalyptus oil, burnt the wild,
burnt the intractable, weedy, deep-rooted tufts of thistle's purple furze, made
house to come down, trashed, screens slashed, jambs unplumbed, without
doors, made drained porcelain the old forms, gave chip, gave to stain
structure, made gone what touched him, stripped paint, grain of floor, made
gauged the gouge of form, form the firmament fallen, made whiteness
a wall, made framed the fallen lavish tragedian shadow where a picture hung,
made what's left a nail, nib, of shadow, made it mine tongue unto nothing,
made it quite, it query, quietude's quill, that silence : writing : then sirens

I

DREAMT DEAD EDEN

Two years you're dead, and still I write I'm Eden
entire, bed down and force-bloomed in seasons

where flesh, untenable, suffers. Summer touches
everything like metaphor. So nasturtiums furl

their botched silks, weave burn inward : nothing here
dies alone. Endless replicate, grief breeds meaning

until the small utopias fall : love is written thus,
and I the lapse between sign and dignified, Eden

and awful. It writes : I, cinder, I, ash, marrow and ten
blackbirds risen, their thirst, too, shriven from brush-

fire. Husband, nothing has touched me like this. Thighs
ensconce my cock the way a garden decorates a grave, cold

flawless plot, no Adam after you, and to what end?
Come noon, what isn't a snake soft, black as tarmac heat-

mirage? Even roses sold roadside, ocean clutching its
lip where waves stop and salt prospers their loss. I drop

the lyric voice down where heat sequesters the cistern,
comes up only thin rope, a tin bucket : what answer?

The birds' rasp and clamor? They complain like hinges.
Their wings open doors and go nowhere. Skyward's

oven, beneath sun, bakes its flat blue enamel. Though
I can write rain into the picture, hang its eaves-born

susurrus outside the window, though I can make any
thing happen, only the willow's tap-root broods

the fathomless under, the beneath, the where
I can't tell of. Tell me : is pain the garden's only plan?

Pain, and the season failed? If I push words under
ground, their roots clutch and crust, gutter like candles.

Thought tapers and snuffs; its thin wick sizzles. Dead
you die again; I walk the graveyard garden schemata;

it plans assassination, my sex souvenired. Picture me
there, neuter widow-widower, my young man's hands

clasped behind my back for the men who carried you
straight to the graves' horizon knives from so many

stitches, skin patched back like awkward sod, I.V.'s
several white shoots grown from cuttings. So thin.

By the end, breath required not even a mouth. Yes
they had to cut your throat, but don't worry I am

making it beautiful, the tracheotomy's puckered
flesh a flower, your voice drawn out by a thread

honeysuckle giving up its pistil. This is not just
my need to control the image : I author this Eden

to keep you near. Understand? Outside, the real garden
withers, too; the door warps and on the hottest days

won't let me out of the lyric, which can't keep anything
alive. I'll tell you how I feel : fuck the real. When I write

butterfly, it's not ironic. It's a sweet name for a needle.

EDEN—*PLEASURE*

—"To be closed (of eyes or lips)" is—
mystery.

How many times then

was he secrecy to me?, Adam kissed, closed

as he was of thighs, so close and hipped

thick like roses, and was not knowledge

greater for its eventual opening?, a rose

not a rose but a metaphor thumbed up

and forefingered, the foreskin's calyx first

slicked back and thus blood crowning

the flower full :

what work does death do

in the dark that I haven't already done?

Tell me : How many times was mystery

dying for it, and each time I went down

on it, didn't I?, "closed of eyes and lips,"

to cradle, crib and seed like silt, to bury

blood in my mouth and rise up a garden...

BURNT TEXT

—*after Archilochos*

His body not pastoral

Fragment—musculature

Suggests the word

Slur : curving a phrase

To completion—yet not

Knowable whole, as flesh

Descends[*and here*

The paper burnt]curl

Hung in curl, damp[*and here*

The speaker whispers

Anatomy]please[*and here*

The paper]plexus[*between*

Fingers]pubis[*whispers*

Please]shadow down

THE EDEN OF THE AUTHOR OF SLEEP

And sleep to grief as air is to the rain,
upon waking, no explanation, just blue

spoons of the eucalyptus measuring
and pouring torrents. A kind of winter.

As if what is real had been buried
and all sure surfaces blurred. Is it me

or the world, risen from beneath?
Mind refining ruin, or an outside

unseen hand, working—as if with
a small brush, for clarity—the details?

To open my eyes is the shape of a city
rising slowly through sand. Cloudy

quartz, my throat, cut unadorned
from the quarry, stone of city cemetery

and roads, to breathe is a mausoleum
breached. To think of Eden is speech

to fill a grave, tree in which knowledge
augurs only its limits, the word *snake*

a thought crawling in the shadow
of its body. Was it, Adam, like this

always, intellect in the mind's small sty
mining confinement for meaning, sleep

to grief as air is to the rain, upon waking,
the world's own weapons turned against it—

EDEN TIRESIAS

[*apocalypsis*—L. to uncover, disclose]

i. "I am the sign of the Letter,/..."

No seed. Flat beneath my hand :
bone. Pelvis a field, but no seed.
Because there was no punishment
like fucking, its whip burned
Adam and nothing after. Because
shine took flight like two parrots
so deep green they seemed black.
And though the field tilted and split
forth meant two ways, though
far into the garden meant I lost
love, even a god could honor that.
"Cell by cell unsexed, I will light the
female," said the snake, and what was
I was lost. What was shine fell;
a shed skin white as water falling.
Wisdom, when did it descend
weeping into each thing? I saw
too much to know who I was :
asleep in each molecule, chaos'
energy. I couldn't speak of this
change, how apocalypse once
gave tongue to each new skin
between my legs, twin parishioners,
bent prayerbooks inside me. *Dominus*
was Eden in me, and the Tree

the world had imagined, except :
interior, what asked for a mind
to hew with wounds. Except memory :
jibe, jilt, jest. What was real died
as its own elegy, as Adam did not.

ii. "…and the designation of the division."

Mons : venus-field held horizon by sharp
fuckless months, field lain fallow. I lost him.
I did not love. Because bitterness lit me
strung tongue to gut. Because god loved
the way the snake shook shine into the tree,
leavening air with matte magnolia leaves.
My mouth opened to ask the snake's name.
Like his tongue from which each word went
each way the meaning bent—leading me
the way back—, I never doubted what I didn't
change down to the syllable, molecule,
shift between dahlia and dalliance, male to
woman, behold, becoming her, became me.
The tree wept cheap greenery; the snake left
what was knowledge, what was the given
matter : until Adam found me again, I put
weeping even inside myself : I knew
I could not explain I saw the end of things
static in anxious limitless rage. It was male,
and yet Adam found me the way language
meant *to uncover* : gladly he lent his mouth,
his hands, husband one, and one lover,
here the church, here the steeple : knuckles knelt,
o Deus, I remember : Self and Other,
and between us every elegy, all the fallen
language that couldn't hold its own

and wouldn't give it back, had no flesh
except how long dust keeps our alphabets.
It came alive outside the mind, intellect.
I loved it. He could not touch me there.

iii. "I am the sign of the Letter,

          and the designation of the division."

No seed. Flat beneath my hand :

          mons : venus-field held horizon by sharp

bone. Pelvis a valley but no seed :

          fuckless months, field lain fallow. I lost him

because there was no punishment

          I did not love. Because bitterness lit me

like fucking, its wicked burn

          strung tongue to gut. Because god loved

Adam and nothing after. Because

          the way the snake shook shine into the tree,

the shine took flight like two parrots,

          leavening air with matte magnolia leaves

so deep green they seemed black.

          My mouth opened to ask the snake's name;

and though the field tilted and split

          like his tongue from which each word went

forth meant two ways, though

          each way the meaning bent—leading me

far into the garden—meant I lost

          the way back, I never doubted what I didn't

love, even a god could honor that.

          "Change down to the syllable, molecule,

cell by cell unsexed, I will light the

          shifts between dahlia and dalliance, male-to-female," said the snake, and what was

        woman, behold, becoming her, became me.
"I" was lost. What was shine fell;

        the tree wept cheap greenery; the snake left
a shed skin white as water falling.

        What was knowledge, what was the given
wisdom, when did it descend into

        matter : until Adam again found me, I put
weeping inside each thing I saw.

        Weeping even inside myself : I knew
too much to know who I was;

        I could not explain I saw the end of things
asleep in each molecule, chaos

        static in anxious limitless rage. It was male
energy. I couldn't speak of this

        and yet Adam found me the way language
changed, how apocalypse once

        meant *to uncover* : gladly he lent his mouth,
gave tongue to each new skin.

        His hands, husband one, and one lover,
between my legs, twin parishioners,

        here the church, here the steeple : knuckles knelt
bent prayerbooks inside me, *Dominus,*

        o Deus, I remember : Self and Other
was Eden in me and the Tree

        between us every elegy, all the falls
the world had imagined except

        language, what couldn't hold its own

interior, what asked for a mind

        and wouldn't give it back, had no flesh

to hew with wounds, no memory

        except how long dust keeps our alphabets.

Jibe, jilt, jest : what was real died as

        it came alive outside the mind, intellect

its own elegy, and Adam did not

        love it.   He could not touch me there.

TORN TEXT

—*after Archilochos*

What damage desires

Text, suffers surface

To abrade, puncture,

lacerate? Here white thighs

And the poem[*here*

The paper deteriorates]

And the body of the poem

[*The paper gets worse*]

Having what mouths

[*Holes*]I cannot forgive

him the elegy[*but here*

The paper is torn]mending

The kiss, sewing cuts inside

OF PARADISE AND THE STRUCTURE
OF GARDENS

Dead said *Let there be a record*,
dead said *Let memory live a little*

longer, dead said *Do not forsake me*,
dead said and said until elegy's voice

stiffened in its vase, his funeral's
last lily. For years I let my voice

thrive—the one live stem left
in that mortuary glass—kept

my thinking pat as obit prose,
platitudinous : I thought

my mind better there than wept,
better elegy than angry

though I'd seen thousands
dead goad moans from men

left behind. Who among us
wasn't historical anymore

among amassed contaminant
bags? Continuous presence,

the history of ideas our common
immunology : I was but one

in a long history of longing
impossibly for the previous,

too young to know elegy touches
nostalgia the way someone was

the last cartographer to ink
an island amid ocean and call it

paradise—during a meanwhile
centuries long, four rivers

ran through it, and dead said
A little longer; Do not forsake me,

dead said. I called him Adam
because him I loved first. Last

lily from his funeral, him I kept
close because all the while

marrow dwindled, faces wasted,
diarrhea, fatigue...For years

I'd refused these facts pertained
to me. I thought the verse line

a boundary between death and life,
a line to control, a repetition, a ritual

I could shape in safety.
In mentalities of earlier times,

a structural link was made—between
happiness and gardens, his cheek

flushed and the live lily
thriving—I'd make the couplet

marry my thinking to centuries,
how the history of ideas runs,

four rivers quiet as lymph :
golden, swollen. Each paradise

was believed real for a time—
Ophir, St. Brendan's Isle, Happy

Isles, Blessed Islands, Kingdom
of Prester John—a common

immunology mapped among fish
and dragons, immense seas, the unknown

a history of longing impossibly
for the previous, shifting farther

offshore as knowledge sailed
farther from the kingdom

and dead said *Let there be*
a record, let memory live a little

longer : long meanwhile, idyllic
elsewhere, walled garden.

III

I called him Adam
because him I loved first.

I call him still because lyric,
like gardens, courts the senses

through form and the couplet
places the rose—along with

the lily and violet—among
the flowers in paradise.

What if he, my brother,
my husband, is a bolted garden,

a boarded well, a fountain
sealed up? Isn't lyric an attempt

to recreate the conditions
of paradise, the marriage bed

I would not yet give up
to the living? What was *pleasure*—

Eden's root—later became
a *hortus conclusus*, paradise

a closed garden. What once was
free became form,

his death, foretold
by the history of ideas :

as paradise shifted farther offshore,
knowledge sailed from theological

kingdoms into the poetic.
Utopias flourished in the gap.

Between the real and what's desired;
between sickbed rags, blood-tinged

scat and colognes, sweat
and cum, who isn't historical

anymore? He died and for years
I went among the living, determined

to be the one cartographer
who could ink an island

IV

among ocean and call it paradise :
though no wolves frightened

our cattle, Adam gave names
to the animals the way an arrow

marries injury to the mortal.
It was the beginning of systems,

each sign given a signified,
placing the rose—along with

the lily and the violet—among
the flowers in paradise.

But back to the roar before
order : so little history, his cheek

flush and the live lily thriving.
Wasn't language one long dying,

one long walling off meaning
from living, a boundary between

death and life, impermeable,
not a repetition of belief, but

the annihilation inherent
in naming, "positive"

and "negative" the way our faces,
inscrutable white surgical masks,

slurred the air above his bed?
Isn't lyric a garden, a conceptual

system whose codes
and complications deny nature,

subject it to force, and shatter it?
Isn't nostalgia how the history

        of ideas quietly keeps our thinking
        occupied, how even elegy mimes

received generic gestures?
Though later the idea of

        the enclosed garden died,
        and paradise lost its wall,

I still wanted for comfort :
many subtle arrangements

        broke with Eden's "simplicity."

        V

        Adam thought tulips too costly

and said of the garden
it was too carefully arranged :

        here you show how art of men
        can purchase nature at a price. Sure.

But I want to keep imagining
the roar before order, before

        words began to leave the forms
        of origin. This isn't nostalgia.

I'm looking for a way
to flourish in the gap,

        to understand *epidemic,*
        epidermis begin *among, on,*

near to, or *in addition*, as in
among people, or *on the skin*.

The thing about the wall is
it kept sin out. The thing

about skin is it keeps
infection out. It's the difference

between *Eden* and *paradise*, a root
derived from pleasure and one

from enclosure; I'm saying
paradise was, at least for a time,

an expression of fear, white slur
masking the air above his bed,

and I'm disgusted I wore that
emblem of institutional paranoia,

contamination, whose root is polluted
touch, the very word taking his skin

away from mine, fear created
by health officials my own fear :

his death was foretold in the move
from etymology to policy : though

many arrangements broke
with Eden's "simplicity,"

I wandered. He wanted for comfort.
I watched and did nothing.

VI

Before theology became poetry,
science worked the garden

for a while, a shift in ideologies,
the gap between sacred

and secular widening until
the sacred fell off the map,

taking his skin away from me.
Scholars wanted to know :

*What kind of apple did Eve eat
and give to Adam?*

As if the empirical were
more important than metaphor.

Despite the gaps, history
never stopped touching us.

It is *because* of the gaps
that he never stops touching me,

I mean, if elegy is a form
his distance from me creates.

I do nothing but work roots
I can't quite see, hoping

a belief in the underneath
of things is needed when

we have to inquire into man's status
in the garden, a subject about which

so much has been written
"paradise might be called,"

a scholar wrote, "a labyrinth
rather than a garden." From God

to man, it is said, the garden
fell, and fell again, its history

one of inquiry because a paradise
is categorically not pleasure

the way a labyrinth is an emblem
of fear to contain the dangerous,

the monstrous birth : it is
the form that keeps

the polluted touch away : for weeks

VII

his diagnosis became my own fear,

but when I asked at the desk
they wanted to know who

was responsible, showed me
to a room where a whitecoat

stripped form from its origins : blood
in vials marked with the possibility

of contaminant. I could feel
pleasure receding, policy's labyrinth

herding what lurked into paradise,
suggesting the logic of creation

changed as language ordered,
dominated the disordered.

My body, like his, became
unknown, to be discovered

not by myself, but by others
bent on knowledge derived

from fear, not care. By then
his mind, divided by fever

and infection. By then, sweat
and shit, the ruin of his skin.

Who touched him touched
with gloves. The garden his body

was fell, and fell again under
the history of empirical inquiry—

needles, medical expense and panic.
Nauseous between knowing and not,

I waited for diagnosis,
and though I received

what the whitecoats called "good
news," we've never not since stopped

living in the gap between
what we know and what we don't,

the notion the poem ties the two
together without killing mystery,

whose face is, after all,
already *closed of eyes or mouth*,

not unlike the dead's. If history
never stops touching us, does it matter

I know a garden, not far
from here, entirely roses?

It was made to be, to mean, only
roses, and the memory of roses,

a form to keep them, to make them
dear : an elegy : a marriage.

VIII

An early interest in botany
and horticulture later affects

the immune system, creates
a weakness in the body's ability

to fight disease that can be
passed on through infection

because the history of ideas
is acquired, and I want to know—

Who is responsible?
I inquired at the front desk.

They showed me to a room
and a whitecoat who asked

questions about my sexual history
the way scholars wanted to know

what kind of apple Eve ate from
and gave to Adam, as if I didn't

already realize the genesis of knowledge
was *among people* the polluted touch.

His policies meant he believed once
the earthly paradise had existed

as a historical reality, but had been
erased from the planet's surface

by people who regarded the garden
as pleasure rather than paradise.

I was at risk as Adam lay dying;
policy said we were putting

everyone at risk, so cartographers
shifted paradise farther offshore,

farther from the kingdom,
moving from theology to poetry

the burden of a history
of a longing for the previous,

and I was too young to understand
he was but one among millions

living the shift. I call him
Adam, but he is long dead,

and dead says *Let there be a record*,
dead says *Let memory live a little*

longer, dead says *Do not forsake me*,
dead says and says and this is

our common immunology :
it has eight sections :

one for each month he lived, dying.

EDEN INCUNABULUM

"As his unlikeness fitted mine"—

so his luciferous kiss, ecliptic : me
      pinned beneath
            lips bitten as under weight of prayer, *Ave*—but
                        no common vocative, no

paradise above, and we not beholden
      to a name, not
            to a local god banking fever blaze his seasonal malady
                      of flowers—nor to demi-urge

nor the lapsarian system's glittering, how
      later we spoke
            between us of sacred and profane as if the numinous
                      could bring death—the only

system—to bear burn outside
      him
            and hang its glister wisdom and singe in the viridian wilt. Lilt,
                      to break salt in that sugar

where skin was no choice
      and sanguine, not
            blameless, though, *Ave*, I loved our words for want
                      beginning liquor, squander

sip and fizz : fuck, ferment
      I loved
             and bluebottles tippling windfall rot, bruises' wicked wine
                  gone vinegar

beneath the taut brief glaze
      of wings, but
             it was not yet nameable, what we later called disease : script
                  brought us by the trick

snake's fakey Beelzebubbery.
      In the dirt
             with his dictionary skin, tight skein of syllables knit by un-
                  numbered undulating

clicking ribs, the snake slunk
      and stung
             and spelled the dust with his tongue and tail and was nothing,
                  a black forked lisp

in the subfusc grass hued
      blue as the blue
             sky tipped its lip to ocean horizon and filled, hugest
                  amphora, and sank,

evening, *Ave*, I will tell you
        now I loved it
                all. That in his hot body there was something similar
                        to the idea of heat

which was in my mind,
        that when we
                alembic, lay together, we bequeathed the white
                        fixed earth beneath

ardent water and a season's kept
        blood, and I not
                a rib of his, not further hurt in his marrow—for the idea
                        of death was in him,

the only system—and we lay together
        in the field
                that was not yet page, not begun with A—, not alpha nor
                        apple, not *Ave*, not yet

because what we knew was
        the least of it
                then. It was difficult to sleep with the love of words gone
                        gospel between my thighs

where nightly he'd jack
             the pulpit, *Ave*
                          Corpus, *Ave* Numen, gnosis and throb unalphabetical,
                                                    I will tell you

I loved it all, fastest brushfires
             and dryburns
                          his body's doublecross, garden lost to loss, incurable
                                          season : wilt, lilt : singe,

our song. And the snake,
             lumen skin
                          of alphabets, rubbing his stomach in the dust until his tin
                                          eyes filled with milk,

his slack skin flickered and split
             and new
                          black sinew out of the slough dead lettered vellum
                                          legless crept and let fall wept

whisper, hiss, paperhush :
             with the skin
                          language left behind I bind time to memorial : Book of Our
                                          Garden Hours, illuminated

bloom : Here a gilt script singe sings of heat

    split in its leaves,

        and the bee gives suck to the book : *Ave* Incunabulum, love's

            first work : *Ave*,

                In Memoriam—

II

CALIFORNIAN

It began like this : a radio
midday, heat—remember?—a shriek

on the highway, and in the yard
Steller's jays chafing over haggle, nag, their claims

a lyric tableau—pretty for the eye—how
sun for months stuck aureoles

of chrome around everything, even
your poems, omens

so no other disaster would happen.
But that there *was* dust—

it had not been so before in June,
grass dead at edges

where a dirt spread had begun, feral
cats interring piss into nasturtiums.

His death had become
the dropped side of a song, melody

undone by damage
exactly the feel of teeth entering

an apple's bruise. The trellis kept
the jasmine rapt

as it collapsed in its own odor; so ardor also
trained the spine

of your weeping into a mind,
confluence of fumes and confusion. Over sills,

jambs, silt sent collusion : thistle, burr, mouse
turds, urine's lingering funk in rooms

where to write was a widow
alone with the last broom she'd bought. Heat,

with its missing finger
and nine filed nails, tuned all afternoon

its blue note : horizon a slack string tautening
against asphalt, whose sound

was drought, marsh departed
before August began, black-outs rolled

house to house, how perfect the fraud and emergencies.
So there were two songs

sung in counterpoint
to jays, argument about belonging to

a place,—remember—
prey and prayer, one struck

the other beneath the lyric image, playing flint
to tinder until on the radio

eastern hills caught fire : extremis,
excelsis, that is

how summer, all veils
and exhalations, courted the hills. How

already the church was burning
when your soul went out to meet him, to marry

his new weather—

TWO ELEGIES CONTAINING FEAR

1—Fragment 42

Not thought, fact

offers patterns : local, habit

of arrangement itself a pleasure

such as the woman each morning scatters

curb-side—crusts thrust in a fist

from a brown bag—gesture

a gist of description : Sapphic fragment, desire's biography

a long day of waiting

the color of pigeon's feathers—

"their hearts grown cold, they slacken their wings"—

and love they are yet

sun-soft asphalt

brushed with sand, each wing-

span unlatched demonstrating tin

chips of glint, the saturation

—like oil—

of plenty,

spectrums—

—FEAR—

Coast woken to
unknown. To think
is verge, surf, shelf

edge. Interior
ocean, mind
a bright cry beached.

Worn porcelain eggshell
ivory and dry, in dilation,
porous, forged

open, the skull's shell
hell in which the sea kneels
tongue—bang

and serenade—, curls
its words' pearls' horde
of whorls. Listen—

waves turn
on their spit, burn
surf, sizzling, stir

the haphazard fat
foam. Listen—
it is certain

emergency. The waves
unravel burning
skeins, skin.

Morning a form

so small

hours like bees house their mouths in darkening wax—amber fast

to umbra—, its way of being

to be smallest

in simile : ivy

weaving between slats

sleaves, sleak, of verdigris and deeper

green; just there in the window

the word *lavation*—slow

imitation of water (wash

and scour, wash

and scour), light lending the hour

density; "I am in two minds"

while reading—the mind

the bird outside the window;

each sentence

its shadow falling in the house—the page

                              and a voice breaking

above it, who is it

                    enters, who is it

CALIFORNIAN

You want to go back
where grief was perfect weather...

A long time
rain trussed the perspectives

with rope and silver. In the grove,
in the eucalyptus,

shadow bound
in shapeless sheaves : a sfumato of indigo

and graphite leaving the air
beneath the leaves a stain, as of mineral

and berries, a smear of menthol.
No birds ever—

or it seems so now—
in the forest. No sound

but a soft mathematics in the branches,
rain adding rain

to rain. No growth—
each tree's dermis : dark blown glass and a breath

kept inside. And fastened
with twists of thin wire

to the branches, the leaves' useless
ruined currency;

it glisters :
a mint of flattened nickels. It seems

you have come back—but
the money of your elegies is no good here,

listen : it isn't your pennies any longer
hold his eyes closed.

TO OTHER LIGHT

Of persons Outside Windows —
The entering — takes away —
E.D.

At the end of mourning : a bookstore

where you begin to read your own life as a story

without plot or drama, self a sky pale with drought

and time passing like that : cloudless, ground

a wide flat span without shadow, sun

occluding the garden in a bright stun of months . . .

After mourning : the scour of hours

at work on the mind. Not what comes clean,

not the enigma of mourning, nor the enigma

of his beauty, its diminishing finish : not to suffer

more, but finally to suffer a clarity in language sufficient

to pain : not in itself the world : the thought of it.

I. USED BOOKS & RECORDS : *Mourning and Melancholia*

Lining the storefront, two plate glass windows,

enormous. As if upon a screen, what occurred outside

a quotation, a version : not quite experience. As if

the real had happened once in the past—

the wind a repetition without sound;

trash in the gutters; the clothes of passersby;

the word "passersby" only something thought

while watching. Strange to leave the store

after closing. Looked at from the street,

through glass : the life of the interior

a descent of light into lateral shadow : your life

removed from consequence until it darkened.

II. USED BOOKS & RECORDS : *The Lives of the Saints*

The boredom of being made an example :

saints, their bodies, offered blade or flame :

exemplary. A rhetoric of hallowing, harrowing

unto death, pages of gilt haloes flaking,

what should've been grotesque, gorgeous :

pierced/hacked/gored with sores : all poreless

artifice. Porcelain : the bloodied/breastless/flood-lunged

skin : an effigy of skin : though he too wasted

suffocated/sarcomaed/thrush-tongued/blinded

in one eye/as if all the world's affliction

his : *no saint*, he said, *no exit to heaven* : still

no grimace without God in it.

To follow in thought
the beloved into death?

To stop. At panic?
At limit? After words.

Un, non, null : knowledge
of death, late spring gone

beyond missing : a mind
to push through image?

Flawed, to attempt
the visible. Not one man ever

dead into sight. The mind
intended toward this, his

shape : how strange,
to proceed without vision.

IV. USED BOOKS & RECORDS : *The Gnostic Religion*

A summer totally allegory : brown-outs, drought,

energy fraud, water rationing.

Customers startled by the back room—

lined to the ceiling with shelves—

suddenly lightless. Then : crappy flashlights

dimly drifting aisle to aisle.

The story the Gnostics told?

The "soul" : in the material dark : just light

to other light. If the ideal soul *is*

indeed wisdom. If nothing more

than the lit pittance given,

flickering. What knowledge they,

desiring. What rumors to be Truth.

v. Elegiac action : to wait

The mock orange : failed blossoms, a weakly fetid smell.

April : jasmine by the back door; nasturtiums turning

in wind. Wilt, wither, and burn, June, and none of it

metaphor. Fourth month without rain, August : awful

powdery texture drought lends everything.

Heat's immense lens : to suffer summer

like that. To pretend to find it meaningful.

VI. USED BOOKS & RECORDS : *The Nag Hammadi Library*

A theological vision :

seeing through lack to what lies behind it,

in gaps of gospel as beyond glass :

summer trees leaning

true : behind the world :

his words, some sweet semblance of himself?

Or what the Gnostics said? : a veil

between wisdom and the world.

And no voice saying.

VII. Elegiac action : to eclipse

Drought : to seem dead
especially. September :

the tongue a loan of dust;
candlelight more true;

the shadow in matter
more evident; being

a darkness forced upon us.
The primary text : doubt

or death? To candle
the shadowed moon;

to tinge and flicker
there hugely? Or

to camera?, as in
September : aperture

and hinge and seeming
swinging shut.

VIII. USED BOOKS & RECORDS : *Writing the Disaster*

In the deep meanwhile

of your life, what was wordless, what passed as fact :

late summer outside the windows :

dim doors struggling shut; wind

an umbrella open against dull sun;

to keep them clean, all the small dogs in sweaters;

all the theories of the real :

a ruin somehow intact. Meanwhile

light might or might

not have; the door; its metal bell.

Meanwhile : the spectacular disaster

of the actual.

IX. ELEGIAC ACTION : TO FUCK

Yes, the world
there : mattress

on the floor,
candle in a dish,

his thighs whiter
for their dark hair :

a surfeit, that surface :
his glasses, water glass,

shoes ordered
by the door.

One thing : how
lyric lets memory

into the present—
his khaki pants

twisted in sheets
like *that*—

        another,
where elegy leads.

The world : never.
Never his hands

forcing your back
to follow its own

arc; muscle looser
under thrust;

his cock rocking
like tide caught

in a lock and
rising for passage—

coupled : as light
to light, so

the touched
to the touching . . .

X. USED BOOKS & RECORDS : *I and Thou*

Sensation of time passing

without him : moth wings' gray powder

on the fingers, regret

the understudy of capture, its dun

brief stain...

And summer nigh to autumn

only early dimming sun

posed just so above brick

and verdigris; awnings furled

and green hoses unrolling slo-mo; sting

of bleach bringing tears; the clean tile floor;

just before closing, a man's face leaning

into the darkening window as if squinting to see

or speak :

"When I was your age
I thought about death

constantly   New York
I had just moved   I lived alone

My job was difficult

and I would sleep on the subway
to and from work   Sometimes

I would miss my stop

and wake up   as if in the middle
of a dream   somewhere I had no

name for   I thought about death
the way people do at your age

sleeping on the subway so often

I dreamt about it   Harsh light
cars rocking the dim

anonymous crush of people

A year of this alone   So I read
books like the one you're reading now

thinking   on the subway home

I was not   am not
a religious person

I was visited by a vision

All noise ceased and though
the car continued to sway

we did not stop   It occurred

I was not inside
my body   could not feel

though I knew things
the way one does in dreams

It was no dream   Across

from where my body
sat   a woman slowly

flickered   her handbag
her flats   expressionless

when she disappeared

I knew she had died

and the same thing
would happen to each passenger

and the car would keep going

Its back-and-forth
like a cradle

is what time feels like

No one was alarmed

It was quiet
and pleasantly warm

I was not surprised
when my own body

began to flicker

I was not   surprised

I was not

there"

CALIFORNIAN

The sea begins in regards
to your questions, whitecaps in late high sun

acetylene from shore to where horizon, deft, ends
troughs

in brighter gesture, severance edged with foam. Where,
if the world is flesh, to place the limit

between your body
and the world? You hate the word

"God" : a beach's bleach
season : a pause between winter and elsewhere. In the firmament's hiatus, gulls'

cries drive
toward promontories the tide : on granite, spindrift

rifted, foam on dark rock stark,
white

sweat on a horse's flank. Call it muscle or salt, still sea
rides land

like that. Though God is no mind—
water crawling

into shell—nor shadow
fast toward shore over water, in regards to the matter, if it please you : ask after
    the rain.

Mussels gulls brought to drop on rock
split, shrug off their hinge

interiors; tide goads
stone, as waves

retreat beneath, to sigh, as if matter were bitter several skins through, or :
write,

if you like.
A lyric has no mind

it wouldn't barter for certainty. Arabesque, error : metaphor is doubt
of a kind :

of two minds : of being
asking after one who has died, and the lighthouse

shunting its white eye in fog, its voice
an order of inquiry

of no color or echo.
As for the rain

gulls drive inland to drop on rock—it shivers
on granite, spread silver

interior spilled. As for your mind
      years now, it seems, out at sea : null spun from fog, it's zero

visibility
to the core, shore an answer precisely beyond the limit

of vision :
it begins in regards. It hears

the white voice trolling its borders...

NOTES

What follows is in recognition of what texts have influenced the poems, as well as to indicate what of those texts, when possible, has been borrowed or outright stolen. In the case of those authors whose work I've drawn on unconsciously, and thus have been unable to honor by naming here: thank you.

Note: all etymologies are from the *Oxford English Dictionary*.

~

The book's epigraph is taken from Duncan's poem "The Law I Love is Major Mover," found in *The Opening of the Field* (Grove Press, 1960).

"Dead House Sonnet": The poem owes its inception and refrain to Alice Notley's poem "Haunt," published in *The Best American Poetry 2002* (Scribner, 2002).

I

"The Eden of the Author of Sleep": The entire poem owes its debt to Hans Jonas' *The Gnostic Religion* (Beacon Press, 1963), especially the chapter "Gnostic Imagery and Symbolic Language." The last line is a direct borrowing. The poem is dedicated to Jean Valentine.

"Burnt Text": The poems "after Archilochos" owe their conception to Guy Davenport's translations, *Carmina Archilochi: The Fragments of Archilochos* (University of California Press, 1964). Some imagery and typography is suggested by or borrowed from his translations.

"Eden Tiresias": The titles of each section are phrases borrowed from the Gnostic hymn, "Thunder: Perfect Mind," from James Robinson's *The Nag Hammadi Library* (Harper & Row, 1988). The snake as vehicle of transformation is where the Gnostics' Eden and Ovid's Tiresias overlap—here, I take a cue from the certain Gnostic cults who read the snake in the garden as a manifestation of Sophia, or Wisdom, the feminine divine.

"Torn Text": owes a debt of phrasing to Robert Duncan's "The Collage, Passages 6" in *Bending the Bow* (New Directions, 1968).

"Eden Incunabulum": An incunabulum is a book printed at an early date (esp. before 1501). The first line is from Tennyson's *In Memoriam*; some passages are borrowed from the alchemical treatise *The Bosom Book of Sir George Ripley*, collected in *Collectanea Chemica*, edited by A.E. Waite (The Alchemical Press, 1991).

"Of Paradise and the Structure of Gardens" is essentially a collage, and could not have been written without Jean Delumeau's *History of Paradise: The Garden of Eden in Myth and Tradition* (Continuum, 1995). Much of the poem is borrowed, stolen and/or misquoted from his text, as well as the texts he habitually refers to.

II

"Californian (It began like this : a radio)" was written in response to a prompt by the poet C.D. Wright and is dedicated to her.

"Two Elegies Containing Fear": Sappho's fragments 42 and 51 are David Campbell's translations, found in the Loeb Classical Library edition of *Greek Lyric* (Harvard University Press, 1982).

"To Other Light": Phrasing in the first, unnumbered section is indebted to

Kristeva's *Black Sun: Depression and Melancholia* (Columbia University Press, 1989), especially the gorgeous fourth chapter, "Beauty: the Depressive's Other Realm." Half the section titles contain books bought and read while working at Wessex Books: I., Sigmund Freud; IV., Hans Jonas; VI., James Robinson; VIII., Maurice Blanchot; and X., Martin Buber. Phrasing in section six is borrowed from the first letter of Heloise to Abelard, in *Letters of Abelard and Heloise* (Penguin, 1974), while section nine is indebted to Merleau-Ponty's *The Visible and the Invisble* (Northwestern University Press, 1968), especially the fourth chapter, "The Intertwining—The Chiasm."

"Californian (The sea begins in regards)": Again, phrasing suggested by the fourth chapter of *The Visible and the Invisible*; a few lines are direct borrowings. The poem is dedicated to Brenda Hillman.

ABOUT THE AUTHOR

A former Stegner Fellow at Stanford University, BRIAN TEARE is the recipient of poetry fellowships from the National Endowment for the Arts and the MacDowell Colony. He has published poetry and criticism in *American Poetry Review, Boston Review, Ploughshares, St. Mark's Poetry Project Newsletter, Seneca Review, Verse,* and *VOLT,* as well as in the anthologies *Legitimate Dangers: American Poets of the New Century* and *At the Barriers: The Poetry of Thom Gunn.* His books and chapbooks include *The Room Where I Was Born, Sight Map, Transcendental Grammar Crown* and ↑. On the graduate faculty of the University of San Francisco and Mills College, he lives in San Francisco, where he makes books by hand for his micropress, Albion Books.

Ahsahta Press

SAWTOOTH POETRY PRIZE SERIES

Ahsahta Press

NEW SERIES

MODERN AND CONTEMPORARY POETS OF THE AMERICAN WEST SERIES

Many of the books in this series are available for download at
http://scholarworks.boisestate.edu/ahsahta/

This book is set in Apollo MT type with Eurostile LT Std titles
by Ahsahta Press at Boise State University
and printed by Thomson-Shore, Inc.
Cover design by Quemadura.
Book design by Janet Holmes.

AHSAHTA PRESS

2010

JANET HOLMES, DIRECTOR
JODI CHILSON, MANAGING EDITOR

KAT COE

CHRIS CRAWFORD

TIMOTHY DAVIS

CHARLES GABEL

KATE HOLLAND

GENNA KOHLHARDT

BREONNA KRAFFT

MATT TRUSLOW

ZACH VESPER

EVAN WESTERFIELD